THE SCHOOL FOR HUSBANDS

ALSO BY RICHARD WILBUR

JEAN BAPTISTE POQUELIN DE

THE SCHOOL
FOR HUSBANDS

COMEDY IN THREE ACTS, 1661

TRANSLATED INTO ENGLISH VERSE
AND INTRODUCED BY

RICHARD WILBUR

HARCOURT BRACE JOVANOVICH, PUBLISHERS
NEW YORK   SAN DIEGO   LONDON

Printed in the United States of America

HBJ

for Brian Bedford

THE SCHOOL FOR HUSBANDS

INTRODUCTION

Molière was devotedly familiar, all his life, with the *commedia dell'arte*, that form of Italian popular comedy in which stock characters like Pantalone (an amorous old miser) and Arlecchino (a foolish servant) improvised their scenes within skeletal plot outlines or "scenarios." During his thirteen years of touring in the provinces, Molière without question saw and learned from those commedia troupes which, in the seventeenth century, traveled to all of the centers of Europe; and his biographer Grimarest says that the company which he brought to Paris in 1658 was "trained to extemporize short comic pieces in the manner of the Italian actors." When, in that year, he pleased the Court with his farce *Le Docteur amoureux*, and secured the patronage of the King's brother, his Troupe de Monsieur was given the use, for half of each week, of the Salle du Petit-Bourbon, sharing that theatre with a resident Italian company headed by the great commedia actor Tiberio Fiorelli. Contemporary accounts tell us that it was a happy association, and that Molière never missed one of Fiorelli's performances.

An admiring indebtedness to Italian comedy, outweighing all other influences, can be seen throughout Molière's plays and entertainments, but seems to me particularly visible in his early success *The School for Husbands* (1661). The single setting of the play is that public square, with its clustered houses or "mansions," which was the traditional backdrop of commedia performances. The action recalls the commonest of commedia plots, in which the *innamorati* or young lovers, balked by their elders and aided by clever servants, manage to outwit their oppressors and marry. As for the characters, Sganarelle is one of Molière's quirky Pantalones, and Lisette and Ergaste are French cousins of those *zanni* who, in the Italian comedy, represented impudent servants with a taste for intrigue.

The School for Husbands, however, is a firmly constructed, fully written play in the high mode of verse comedy. Nothing is left to improvisation. Such a farcical bit as Valère's and Ergaste's accosting of the oblivious Sganarelle (I, 3), which in commedia would give the actors

1

all sorts of inventive latitude, is here wholly worded and choreo-
graphed by the dialogue and stage directions. The chief persons of the
play, though behind them loom certain stock figures, are variously
individuated by Molière's art and endowed with a measure of complex-
ity. In the first act of *Husbands*, we meet two middle-aged brothers,
Sganarelle and Ariste, who have promised a dying friend to rear, and
perhaps ultimately to marry, his two orphaned daughters. Ariste, an
easygoing man of fifty-nine or so, has treated his spirited ward, Léonor, in a considerate and indulgent fashion, thus gaining her grateful
affection. Sganarelle, Ariste's junior by twenty years, is a premature
fuddy-duddy who has raised his charge, Isabelle, with a domineering
strictness, and it will of course be the business of the play to rescue
her from his tyranny and unite her with her romantic young neighbor,
Valère. Certain peculiarities of Sganarelle (whose central part was
originally played by Molière himself) are conveyed in the play's early
scenes: his cranky opposition to fashion and to urban social pleasures,
his extolling of ancestral ways and standards, his crusty bad manners,
his mistrustfulness, his ill-will toward Ariste. All these things, as the
second and third acts proceed, become intelligible aspects of his
psychology.

As Albert Bermel has noted, the second act — in which the cause
of Isabelle is advanced by a series of clever deceptions and dodges —
has a number of surprises for us. Isabelle, who in Act I was a poor
victim with but twenty-nine syllables to say, emerges in Act II as a
mettlesome, resourceful young woman who, horrified by the prospect
of marriage to a bully, drives all the action by improvising one ruse
after another. It is surprising, too, that the enamored Valère and his
canny valet, Ergaste, who at the end of the first act retired to ponder
stratagems, are in the second reactive at best, their behavior being
largely confined to the divining of Isabelle's purposes and the abetting
of her initiatives. When the figures of a play behave in unexpected and
yet credible ways, it increases their dimensionality, and here it is above
all the unanticipated actions of Sganarelle which serve to build com-
plex character. The suspicious man of Act I becomes, in Act II,
utterly gullible; the harsh guardian becomes a doting dispenser of pet
names; the possessive husband-to-be develops a maudlin sympathy
for his young rival. Out of these apparent contradictions we assemble
a portrait of an anxious, alienated man, resentful of his brother's
sociable aplomb and out of touch with people in general — a man who,

significantly, can be blind to others when they are present (I, 3) and can fancy them present when they are not ("Who goes there? Ah, I'm dreaming.") His outlandish views and posturings are intended, we perceive, to confer a style upon his isolation and, as Lionel Gossman says, to impress the world by a claim of superiority to it. In his grandiose insecurity, Sganarelle cannot allow others their freedom and their differences; his relation to the world consists in berating it, and in demanding of others that they regard him as a model and embody his values. It is not, after all, surprising that so shaky and fantastic a man should be disarmed by the feigned docility of Isabelle, and duped by the flatteries of Valère.

But the play, as we experience it, is not always busy with the revelation of personality; it is also, and perhaps more densely, concerned with portraying the intricacies of communication in an atmosphere of intrigue—with suspicion, deception, implication, inference, double entendre, the understanding or misunderstanding of look or word. In the latter part of Act II, Scene 2, for example, Isabelle has asked Sganarelle to convey an ambiguous message which she intends as a signal to Valère that she is aware of his passion; Sganarelle understands the message as a stern rebuff, and delivers it with an admixture of his own jealous vehemence; Valère does not know what to make of this filtered communication, sent by his beloved but spoken by his rival; Ergaste, however, hypothesizes a secret and favorable meaning, and the departing Sganarelle, looking back at Ergaste and Valère in colloquy, more than once misreads the latter's facial expressions. Given so rich a fabric of doubtful interactions, a critic might well classify *School for Husbands* as "comedy of intrigue," and many have done so. Others have as firmly called it "comedy of character." Some have treated it as a hybrid transitional piece—an anticipation of deeper character studies to come, or a sketch for *The School for Wives* (1662), which would return to its theme and rework certain of its situations. Yet it seems to me that we may find this play quite sufficient in its own right, judging with Jacques Guicharnaud that its balance of elements is "esthetically satisfying"; with Donald Frame that it represents Molière's "first demonstration of complete mastery of his craft"; with Martin Turnell that, whatever its place in the canon, it is a "constant delight."

The title of *School for Husbands* may seem to imply that the play is a lecture, in which the author advocates permissive child-rearing and

3

the laissez-faire treatment of young women and wives. Certainly the comedy appealed to the ladies of Molière's day, whose enthusiasm was a great factor in its success; and as surely there will be those who, presenting it in this translation, will be tempted to give it a strong feminist spin. They will be the more inclined to do so because Ariste, whom some have taken to be Molière's spokesman, is rewarded by the plot with the fond fidelity of Léonor. Still, it is well to remember that the *raisonneurs* of Molière are never effectual or wholly admirable in their arguments, and that their major function is to play straight man to the aberrated central figure, exacerbating him and prompting him to display his imbalance. It is an impoverishment, furthermore, to treat a dramatic character as a mere mouthpiece, and readers should bear in mind that Ariste's views and actions are conditioned by the desire of an aging man to retain the goodwill of a lively, beautiful young woman. We should also recognize that Isabelle, though driven by circumstances to hoodwink her guardian, is not at all a social rebel. Neither she nor Léonor shares the servants' relish for amorous trickery; she repeatedly asks the audience, in asides or little soliloquies, to excuse her subterfuges; and in her letter to Valère she regrets being forced "to overstep the bounds of decorum prescribed for my sex." There is no question, in *School for Husbands*, as to where our sympathies are to lie, but the play seems less a positive case for specific freedoms than a depiction of oppressive folly. If we look in this work for Molière's "ideas," we can most confidently do so by focusing on Sganarelle: in him, as in the Orgon of *Tartuffe*, we see that it is wrong, and deserving of ridicule, to misuse one's authority as parent or husband, and that—on the comic stage at least, where Nature tends to triumph—such tyranny will bring about its own undoing.

This French play, now 330 years old, is like Molière's work generally in requiring little or no mediation; it comes across to us readily, in spite of time and cultural differences. But the reader may be amused by this footnote, which I take from Von Laun's old prose translation, and which has to do with the royal edict brought on stage by Sganarelle at the beginning of Act II, Scene 6. "It is remarkable that Louis XIV, who was so extravagant himself in his buildings, dress, and general expenses, published sixteen laws against luxury; the law Sganarelle speaks of was promulgated November 27th, 1660, against the use of *guipures, cannetilles, paillettes*, etc., on men's dresses." Sganarelle's speech, then, is topical; and since it praises the King's

[*Introduction*]

decree through the lips of a crank, it may be one of those passages in which Molière felt free to josh his royal or noble patrons with a jester's impunity.

In working on this translation, I have been helped at times by the prose versions of Baker and Miller, of Wall, and of Von Laun. My wife, as always, has been my chief consultant. I must also thank Jean Migrenne, William Jay Smith, Sonja Haussmann Smith, and Albert Bermel for their clarifications of particular passages, and James Merrill for his kindness in reading the whole.

R. W.
Cummington
May, 1991

5

CHARACTERS

SGANARELLE, a man approaching forty; brother to Ariste and guardian to Isabelle

ARISTE, Sganarelle's elder brother by twenty years; guardian to Léonor

ISABELLE, Léonor's sister, Sganarelle's young ward

LÉONOR, Isabelle's sister and Ariste's ward

LISETTE, Léonor's maid

VALÈRE, Isabelle's lover

ERGASTE, valet to Valère

A MAGISTRATE

A NOTARY

The scene throughout: a residential square in Paris

First produced by the Old Globe Theatre, San Diego, California, in January 1992

ACT 1

SCENE ONE

SGANARELLE, ARISTE

SGANARELLE

Enough talk, Brother; let's give our tongues a rest,
And let's each live his life as he thinks best.
Although you're my superior in age
And old enough, indeed, to be a sage,
Nevertheless I hereby notify you
That I don't care to be corrected by you,
That my own taste suffices to advise me,
And that my way of life quite satisfies me.

ARISTE

Yet all condemn it.

SGANARELLE

             Yes, idiots of your sort,
Dear Brother.

ARISTE

             Thank you; what a sweet retort!

[*Act One* · *Scene One*]

SGANARELLE

Since you won't drop the subject, tell me, do,
What these fine critics take exception to.

ARISTE

They blame that surly humor which makes you flee
From all the pleasures of society,
And lends a sort of grim outlandishness
To all you do, even to the way you dress.

SGANARELLE

I see: I mustn't wear what clothes I please,
But must submit to fashion's wise decrees!
Do you propose, by precepts so bizarre,
Dear elder brother—for that is what you are
By twenty blessed years, I must confess,
Although of course it couldn't matter less—
Do you propose, I say, to force me to
Adorn myself as your young dandies do?
To wear those little hats which leave their brains,
Such as they are, exposed to winds and rains,
And those immense blond wigs which hide their features
And make one doubt that they are human creatures?
Those tiny doublets, cut off at armpit-level,
Those collars hanging almost to the navel,
Those sleeves that drag through soups and gravy boats,
And those huge breeches, loose as petticoats?
Those small, beribboned slippers, too neat for words,
Which make them look like feather-footed birds?
Those rolls of lace they force their legs to wear
Like the leg irons that slaves and captives bear,
So that we see each fop and fashion plate

12

[*Act One · Scene One*]

Walk like a pigeon, with a waddling gait?
You'd have me dress like that? I note with loathing
That you're attired in just such modish clothing.

ARISTE

It's best at all times to observe convention
And not, by being odd, attract attention.
For all extremes offend, and wise men teach
Themselves to deal with fashion as with speech,
Accepting calmly, with no fuss or haste,
Whatever changes usage has embraced.
I'm far from recommending those whose passion
Is always to improve upon the fashion,
And who are filled with envy and dismay
If someone else is more extreme than they:
But it is bad, on any ground, to shun
The norm, and not to do the thing that's done;
Better by far to join the foolish throng
Than stand alone and call the whole world wrong.

SGANARELLE

There speaks a vain old man who slyly wears
A black wig to conceal his few white hairs.

ARISTE

It's strange with what persistence and ill grace
You throw my age forever in my face,
And how incessantly I'm forced to hear
You blame my style of dress and my good cheer;

13

[*Act One · Scene One*]

As if old age should bid all joys good-bye,
Thinking of nothing save that it must die,
And doesn't look grotesque enough unless
It's sour of mood and dismal in its dress.

SGANARELLE

However that may be, my firm intent
Is not to alter my habiliment.
Despite the mode, I'll have a hat that's made
To shield my head and give my eyes some shade,
A fine long doublet which will wrap me 'round
To warm my belly and keep digestion sound,
Breeches which fit me well in thighs and seat,
And sturdy shoes which won't torment my feet.
Thus did our forebears dress, and they were wise;
Those I offend are free to shut their eyes.

SCENE TWO

LÉONOR, ISABELLE, LISETTE; ARISTE AND SGANARELLE,

TALKING UNOBSERVED AT THE FRONT OF THE STAGE.

LÉONOR, *to Isabelle*

I'll take the blame, if he should make a scene.

LISETTE, *to Isabelle*

Shut in your lonely room all day? How mean!

ISABELLE

He's like that.

LÉONOR

Sister, I'm sorry for your plight.

LISETTE, *to Léonor*

His brother and he are just like day and night.
Madam, the Fates were kind in giving you,
As guardian, the sane one of the two.

[*Act One · Scene Two*]

ISABELLE

I marvel that for one day he should fail
To drag me with him, or shut me in my jail.

LISETTE

I'd send him and his Spanish ruff to Hades,
If —

SGANARELLE, *Lisette having bumped into him*

Where are you going, may I ask, young ladies?

LÉONOR

We don't yet know, but since the weather's fair
I've asked my sister out to take the air,
And —

SGANARELLE, *to Léonor*

You may go where you like, for all of me.
Just run along. (*Pointing to Lisette:*) She'll keep you company.
(*To Isabelle:*)
But you, if you please, won't go on this excursion.

ARISTE

Oh, Brother, let them go. They need diversion.

SGANARELLE

Your servant, Brother.

ARISTE

Youth must be permitted —

SGANARELLE

Youth, Sir, is foolish; and age can be half-witted.

ARISTE

With Léonor, could she come to any ill?

SGANARELLE

No; but with me she will be safer still.

ARISTE

But —

SGANARELLE

All that she does I strictly oversee,
Thus honoring my responsibility.

ARISTE

And do I neglect her sister, would you say?

SGANARELLE

Well, each man thinks and acts in his own way.
These girls are orphans. Their father, our dear friend,
Entrusted them to us at his life's end,
Bidding us marry them, if so inclined,

Or find them spouses of a proper kind.
Thus we have ruled them with the double sway
Of father and husband, from their childhood's day.
That one, dear Brother, you undertook to rear,
And I took charge of raising this one, here;
Pray govern yours according to your views,
And let me train the other as I choose.

ARISTE

I think—

SGANARELLE

I think, and firmly will declare,
That that's how we should manage this affair.
You let your charge be dashingly arrayed:
So be it; she has a flunky and a maid:
I'm quite content; she idly gads about,
And our young beaux are free to seek her out:
All that is splendid. But my charge, be it known,
Shall live by my desires, and not her own;
She'll dress in serge, in simple browns and grays,
And not wear black except on holidays;
Like any prudent girl, she'll stay indoors
And occupy herself with household chores;
In leisure time she'll mend my linen, or make
Some knitted stockings for amusement's sake;
She'll close her ears to young men's fancy talk,
And never go unguarded for a walk.
The flesh is weak, as each day's gossip warns.
If I can help it, I shall not wear horns,
And since her destiny's to be my wife,
I mean to guard her as I would my life.

[*Act One · Scene Two*]

ISABELLE

You have no reason —

SGANARELLE

       Be still. You know you're not
To leave the house without me. Had you forgot?

LÉONOR

Oh, come, Sir —

SGANARELLE

       Madam, I'd rather not debate
With one whose wit and wisdom are so great.

LÉONOR

Are you vexed to find me here with Isabelle?

SGANARELLE

Why yes — because you spoil her, truth to tell.
Frankly, your visits here disturb my peace,
And you'd oblige me if they were to cease.

LÉONOR

Well, shall I speak with equal frankness, Sir?
I don't know how all this may sit with her,
But such mistrust, I know, would rouse my ire;
And, though we share a mother and a sire,
We're not true sisters if the things you do,
Day after day, can make her fond of you.

LISETTE

Yes, all these stern precautions are inhuman.
Are we in Turkey, where they lock up women?
It's said that females there are slaves or worse,
And that's why Turks are under Heaven's curse.
Our honor, Sir, is truly very frail
If we, to keep it, must be kept in jail.
But do you think that such severities
Bar us, in fact, from doing what we please,
Or that, when we're dead set upon some plan,
We can't run rings around the cleverest man?
All these constraints are vain and ludicrous:
The best course, always, is to trust in us.
It's dangerous, Sir, to underrate our gender.
Our honor likes to be its own defender.
It almost gives us a desire to sin
When men mount guard on us and lock us in,
And if my husband were so prone to doubt me,
I just might justify his fears about me.

SGANARELLE, *to Ariste*

Well, teacher, there's what comes of what you teach.
Do you not shudder, hearing such a speech?

ARISTE

Brother, we should but smile at her discourse.
And yet her notions have a certain force:
All women like a bit of freedom, and
It's wrong to rule them with a heavy hand.
It isn't bolts and bars and strict controls
That give our wives and maidens virtuous souls;
No, honor keeps their feet on duty's path,

And not our harshness or our threatened wrath.
I say, indeed, that there's no woman known
Who's good and faithful through constraint alone.
We can't dictate a woman's every move:
If we're to sway her, it must be by love,
And I, whatever curbs I'd put upon her,
Would not feel safe were I to trust my honor
To one who was deterred from wronging me
Only by lack of opportunity.

SGANARELLE

What drivel!

ARISTE

   As you like; but still I say
That we should school the young in a pleasant way,
And chide them very gently when they've erred,
Lest virtue come to seem a hateful word.
I've raised Léonor by maxims such as these;
I've not made crimes of little liberties;
To all her young desires I've given consent —
Of which, thank Heaven, I've no cause to repent.
I've let her see good company, and go
To balls, and plays, and every sort of show,
Such social pleasures being well designed,
I've always held, to form a youthful mind.
The world's a school in which we learn to live
By better lessons than any book could give.
She's fond of buying gowns, and bows, and frills:
Well, what of that? I give her what she wills,
For gay attire's a thing we should permit
Young girls to enjoy, if we can pay for it.
She's pledged to wed me by her father's order,

But I shall not be overbearing toward her:
I well know that, in years, we're far apart,
And so I free her to consult her heart.
If the four thousand crowns I yearly earn,
My deep affection, and my dear concern
Can compensate, in her considered view,
For all the years which separate us two,
Then she shall wed me; if not, she'll choose another.
She might be happier without me, Brother,
And I had rather give her up than see
Her forced, against her will, to marry me.

SGANARELLE

How sweet he is! All sugar and spice! My, my!

ARISTE

Well, that's my nature, thank the Lord, and I
Deplore the too-strict training which has led
So many children to wish their parents dead.

SGANARELLE

The more one lets the young run wild, the greater
A task it is to discipline them later;
You'll view her willful habits with misgiving
When the time comes to change her mode of living.

ARISTE

Why should I change it?

SGANARELLE

Why?

ARISTE

Yes.

SGANARELLE

I don't know.

ARISTE

Is there any disgrace, do you think, in living so?

SGANARELLE

Oh, come! If you marry her, will you still allow
The girlish freedoms you permit her now?

ARISTE

Why not?

SGANARELLE

Then you'll indulge her, I suppose,
In wearing ribbons, beauty spots, and bows?

ARISTE

Of course.

23

SGANARELLE

And let her madly run about
To every ball, or fashionable rout?

ARISTE

Quite so.

SGANARELLE

You'll receive young gallants in your house?

ARISTE

Why, yes.

SGANARELLE

To make merry, and amuse your spouse?

ARISTE

Indeed.

SGANARELLE

And they'll pay her flowery compliments?

ARISTE

No doubt.

[*Act One · Scene Two*]

SGANARELLE

And you'll stand by at these events,
Looking entirely unconcerned and cool?

ARISTE

Most certainly.

SGANARELLE

Enough! You're an old fool.
(*To Isabelle:*)
Go in; you mustn't hear such shameful rot.

ARISTE

I'll trust my wife's fidelity, and shall not
Do otherwise, when married, than now I do.

SGANARELLE

How I'll enjoy it when she cuckolds you!

ARISTE

I don't know what the stars intend for me,
But if they should deny you cuckoldry
It won't be your fault, for you've taken great
Pains to deserve that horny-headed state.

SGANARELLE

Laugh on, my jester. It's wondrous to behold
A clown who's almost sixty winters old!

LÉONOR

If he should wed me, I'd never make him bear
The fate of which you speak; to that I'll swear.
But were I forced to wear your wedding ring,
I frankly couldn't promise anything.

LISETTE

We owe fidelity to them that trust us;
But cheating folk like you is simple justice.

SGANARELLE

Just hold your cursèd, ill-bred tongue, d'you hear?

ARISTE

You've brought this mockery on yourself, I fear.
Farewell. Do change your views, and realize
That locking up one's wife can be unwise.
Brother, your servant.

SGANARELLE

      I'm not *your* servant, Brother.
      (*Alone:*)
Oh, but those three are made for one another!
What a fine household! An agèd maniac
With foppish clothing on his creaking back;

26

A girlish mistress who's a wild coquette;
Impudent servants: Wisdom herself would get
Nothing but headaches by attempting to
Correct the ways of that unbalanced crew.
Lest Isabelle, in their loose company,
Should lose the sound ideas she's learned from me,
I'll send her back where she'll be safe from harm
Among the beans and turkeys of my farm.

SCENE THREE

VALÈRE, *at the rear of the stage*

Ergaste, look: there's that Argus I abhor,
The guardian of the girl whom I adore.

SGANARELLE, *thinking himself alone*

It's altogether shocking, the decay
Of manners and of morals in our day!

VALÈRE

I'm going to accost him, if I can,
And strike up an acquaintance with the man.

SGANARELLE, *thinking himself alone*

Where are those standards, stern and absolute,
Which were the basis, once, of good repute?
Our wild young folk indulge their every whim,
And won't . . .
      (*Valère bows to Sganarelle, from a distance*)

VALÈRE

He didn't see me bow to him.

[*Act One · Scene Three*]

ERGASTE

Maybe he's blind on this side; what do you say
We walk around him?

SGANARELLE, *thinking himself alone*

          I must end my stay.
Life in this city only serves to rouse
My worst . . .

VALÈRE, *approaching bit by bit*

       I *must* gain entrance to his house.

SGANARELLE, *hearing a noise*

Did I hear a voice?
(*Thinking himself alone:*) In the country, praise the Lord,
The follies of these times can be ignored.

ERGASTE, *to Valère*

Go up to him.

SGANARELLE, *once more hearing a noise*

      Eh?
      (*Hearing no further sound:*)
         My ears are ringing, I guess.
      (*Thinking himself alone:*)
There, girls have simple pleasures, simple dress . . .
      (*He sees Valère bowing to him.*)
What's this?

[Act One · Scene Three]

ERGASTE, *to Valère*

Get closer.

SGANARELLE, *still staring at Valère*

There, no fops are seen . . .
(*Valère bows to him again.*)
What the devil —
(*He turns and sees Ergaste bowing on the other side.*)
Another? Such bowing! What does it mean?

VALÈRE

Do I disrupt your thoughts, Sir, by this greeting?

SGANARELLE

Perhaps.

VALÈRE

Forgive me; but this happy meeting
Is such a privilege, such a pleasure too,
I couldn't forgo this chance to speak with you.

SGANARELLE

I see.

VALÈRE

And to assure you that I stand
Entirely at your service, heart and hand.

[*Act One · Scene Three*]

SGANARELLE

I'm sure of it.

VALÈRE

It's my happiness to be
Your neighbor, for which I thank my destiny.

SGANARELLE

Well put.

VALÈRE

But now, Sir, have you heard the new
Gossip at court? Some think it may be true.

SGANARELLE

Does that concern me?

VALÈRE

No; but in such a matter
Folk sometimes like to hear the latest chatter.
Shall you go see the lavish preparations
For our new Dauphin's natal celebrations?

SGANARELLE

If I like.

31

[*Act One · Scene Three*]

VALÈRE

Ah, Paris affords us, you must own,
A hundred pleasures which elsewhere are unknown;
The country offers nothing that compares.
What are your pastimes?

SGANARELLE

Tending to my affairs.

VALÈRE

Still, one needs relaxation, and the brain,
From too much serious use, can suffer strain.
What do you do 'twixt supper time and bed?

SGANARELLE

Just what I please.

VALÈRE

Ah, Sir, that's nicely said;
A wise reply; we all should see life thus,
And only do what truly pleases us.
Some evening, if you're free of business, I'll
Drop by, if I may, and chat with you a while.

SGANARELLE

Your servant.

SCENE FOUR

VALÈRE, ERGASTE

VALÈRE

That crackpot! What did you make of him?

ERGASTE

He gives gruff answers, and his manner's grim.

VALÈRE

Oh, I can't bear it!

ERGASTE

What?

VALÈRE

        It irks my soul
That the one I love is under the control
Of a fierce, sharp-eyed dragon who will never
Allow her any liberty whatever.

ERGASTE

Why, that's to your advantage; the situation
Should fill your heart with hope and expectation.

33

Cheer up; you have no cause to feel undone.
A woman closely watched is halfway won,
And a harsh husband or a crabbèd sire
Is just what any lover should desire.
I don't chase women; for that I have no talent;
And I do not profess to be a gallant;
But I've served woman-chasers by the score
Who told me often that nothing pleased them more
Than meeting with those fractious husbands who
Come grumbling home and scold all evening through,
Those brutes who groundlessly mistrust their wives,
Checking on every moment of their lives,
And act proprietary and unpleasant
When young admirers of their wives are present.
"All this," they said, "is favorable to us.
'The lady's pique at being treated thus,
'And the warm sympathy which we then express,
'Can pave the way to amorous success."
In short, if you have hopes of Isabelle,
Her guardian's cranky ways may serve you well.

VALÈRE

But for four months I've been her worshipper,
And never had one chance to speak with her!

ERGASTE

Love makes men clever; but it's not done much for you.
In your place, I'd —

VALÈRE

　　　　　　But what was there to do?
She's never seen without that beast nearby;
There are no servants in his house whom I

[*Act One · Scene Four*]

Could tempt with little gifts, and thus obtain
As helpers in my amorous campaign.

ERGASTE

Then she doesn't know, as yet, of your devotion?

VALÈRE

Well, as to that I have no certain notion.
Whenever that barbarian's taken her out,
She's seen me, for I've shadowed her about
And sought by fervent glances to impart
The raging passion that is in my heart.
My eyes have spoken boldly; but how well
She's understood their language, who can tell?

ERGASTE

Such language can be hard to fathom, when
It's not interpreted by tongue or pen.

VALÈRE

How can I end this anguishing ordeal,
And learn if she's aware of what I feel?
Think of some stratagem.

ERGASTE

                  That's what we must discover.
Let's go inside a while, and think it over.

ACT 2

SCENE ONE

ISABELLE, SGANARELLE

SGANARELLE

That's quite enough; I know the house, and can,
From what you tell me, recognize the man.

ISABELLE, *aside*

O Heaven! be gracious now, and lend your aid
To the artful plot my innocent love has laid.

SGANARELLE

You've learned, I gather, that his name's Valère?

ISABELLE

Yes.

SGANARELLE

    Go then; don't fret; I'll handle this affair.
I'll speak at once to that young lunatic.

ISABELLE, *as she goes in*

It's bold for a girl to play this sort of trick;
But since I'm harshly and unjustly used,
I hope, by all fair minds, to be excused.

SCENE TWO

SGANARELLE, ERGASTE, VALÈRE

SGANARELLE, *at Valère's door*

Well, here's the house. I'll act without delay.
Who goes there? Ah, I'm dreaming . . . Hullo, I say!
It doesn't surprise me, knowing what now I know,
That he paid court to me an hour ago;
But I'll soon dash the hopes of this fond lover —
    (*To Ergaste, who has come out in haste:*)
You clumsy oaf! Do you mean to knock me over?
Why stand there like a post and block the door?

VALÈRE

I regret, Sir —

SGANARELLE

Ah! It's you I'm looking for.

VALÈRE

I, Sir?

SGANARELLE

Yes, you. Your name's Valère, I find.

[*Act Two · Scene Two*]

SGANARELLE

It is.

VALÈRE

A word with you, if you don't mind.

VALÈRE

May I serve you somehow? I should be proud to do —

SGANARELLE

No, but there's something I can do for you,
And that is why I've sought your house, and found you.

VALÈRE

You've come to my house, Sir!

SGANARELLE

Yes. Need that astound you?

VALÈRE

It does indeed, and I'm in ecstasies
At this great honor —

SGANARELLE

Forget the honor, please.

[*Act Two · Scene Two*]

VALÈRE

Won't you come in?

SGANARELLE

I see no need of that.

VALÈRE

I beg you, Sir.

SGANARELLE

I'll stay where I am; that's flat.

VALÈRE

I'd hear you better if we went within.

SGANARELLE

I shall not budge.

VALÈRE

Ah well, I must give in.
(*To Ergaste:*)
Our guest won't enter, but he must have a seat.
Quick, bring a chair.

SGANARELLE

I'll talk to you on my feet.

[*Act Two · Scene Two*]

VALÈRE

But how can I let you —

SGANARELLE

What infernal stalling!

VALÈRE

Such incivility would be appalling.

SGANARELLE

What in the world is more uncivil, pray,
Than not to hear what people want to say?

VALÈRE

I'll do as you wish, then.

SGANARELLE

That's a splendid notion.
(*They go to great lengths of ceremony, in putting on their hats.*)
These courtesies are a waste of time and motion.
Now, will you listen?

VALÈRE

I shall, Sir, with delight.

[*Act Two · Scene Two*]

SGANARELLE

Do you know that I'm the guardian of a quite
Young girl, who's rather pretty; that we dwell
Nearby, and that her name is Isabelle?

VALÈRE

Yes.

SGANARELLE

    I won't say, then, what you know already.
Do you know, likewise, that her charms have led me
To feelings other than a guardian's pride,
And that her destiny is to be my bride?

VALÈRE

No.

SGANARELLE

    Then I tell you so. And I bid you cease
Your warm advances, and leave the girl in peace.

VALÈRE

I, Sir?

SGANARELLE

    You. Don't deny that you pursue her.

[*Act Two · Scene Two*]

VALÈRE

Who told you, then, of my devotion to her?

SGANARELLE

People whose testimony one can credit.

VALÈRE

But who?

SGANARELLE

She herself.

VALÈRE

She?

SGANARELLE

                    She. That's twice I've said it.
That good young woman, who, since she was small,
Has loved me, came just now and told me all,
And charged me, furthermore, to let you know
That when, of late, you've dogged her footsteps so,
Her heart, which your attentions scandalize,
Read all too well the language of your eyes;
That what you feel for her is all too clear,
And that t'will be no use to persevere
In shows of passion which can only be
Offensive to a heart that's pledged to me.

45

[*Act Two · Scene Two*]

You say that she, of her own accord, besought you —

Yes, to convey the message that I've brought you.
She adds that, having plumbed your heart, she would
Have made herself much sooner understood,
If she'd been able, through some messenger,
To express the feelings which arose in her;
At last, in her extreme frustration, she
Had no recourse but to make use of me,
In order to inform you, as I've said,
That I'm the man she loves and means to wed,
That the sheep's eyes you've made were made in vain,
And that, if you have any sort of brain,
You'll take your passion elsewhere. For now, farewell.
I've told you everything I had to tell.

Good heavens, Ergaste, what do you make of this?

How stunned he looks!

              It's my analysis
That you need not be troubled for a minute.
This message has a secret meaning in it,
And wasn't sent by someone who desires
To terminate the love which she inspires.

[*Act Two · Scene Two*]

SGANARELLE, *aside*

He takes it well.

VALÈRE, *sotto voce, to Ergaste*

You think her words implied —

ERGASTE, *sotto voce*

Yes . . . But he's watching us; let's go inside.

SGANARELLE, *alone*

My, what confusion's written on his visage!
Clearly, he didn't expect so harsh a message.
Let me call Isabelle. In her we find
The effect of sound instruction on the mind.
So perfect is her virtue that if a man
Dares look at her, she puts him under ban.

SCENE THREE

ISABELLE, SGANARELLE

ISABELLE, *sotto voce, as she enters*

I fear that, in his passion, my lover may
Not fathom what my message meant to say;
And so I must, since I'm a captive here,
Risk yet another to make my meaning clear.

SGANARELLE

Well, I am back.

ISABELLE

What happened?

SGANARELLE

Your words quite dashed
Your lover's spirits; he's utterly abashed.
He sought to deny his passion, but once he knew
That you had sent me, and that I spoke for you,
The fellow stood there speechless and nonplussed.
He won't be troubling us again, I trust.

[*Act Two · Scene Three*]

ISABELLE

Ah, won't he, though! I greatly fear he will,
And that he'll give us much more trouble still.

SGANARELLE

What grounds do you have for such a premonition?

ISABELLE

You'd hardly left the house upon your mission
When I went to the window for a breath of air
And saw a young man on that corner there,
Who, much to my amazement, shortly came
And greeted me in my admirer's name,
And then, with further impudence, tossed into
My room a box which held a billet-doux.
I would have thrown it back to him, but his feet
Had far too quickly borne him up the street,
Leaving me full of outrage and distress.

SGANARELLE

Just think of it! Such guile, such craftiness!

ISABELLE

Duty requires that I send back again
Both box and letter to this cursèd swain,
But who's to run the errand I cannot say.
I dare not ask you —

SGANARELLE

My sweet, of course you may.
You prove your love of me by what you ask,
And I accept with joy this little task:
I can't express my pleasure.

ISABELLE

Then take this, do.

SGANARELLE

Let's see, now, what he's dared to say to you.

ISABELLE

Oh, Heavens! Don't break the seal.

SGANARELLE

Not open it? Why?

ISABELLE

He'd think 'twas I it had been opened by.
A decent girl should never read the tender
Communications which young men may send her:
To show such curiosity betrays
A secret appetite for flattering praise.
I think it right, then, that this missive be
Returned unopened, and most speedily,
So that Valère will learn this very day
How much I scorn him, and will without delay
Discard the hopes which he's invested in me,
And make no more absurd attempts to win me.

50

[*Act Two · Scene Three*]

SGANARELLE

Her point's well taken; this young girl reasons rightly.
My dear, your virtue and good sense delight me:
My teachings have borne fruit, I see with pride,
And you are worthy indeed to be my bride.

ISABELLE

Still, I won't oppose your wishes; I wouldn't dare to.
You have the letter; open it, if you care to.

SGANARELLE

No, no, your reasons cannot be contested.
I'll go and do this errand you've requested,
Make a brief call nearby — ten minutes at best —
And then return to set your mind at rest.

SCENE FOUR

SGANARELLE, ERGASTE

SGANARELLE, *alone*

It floods my soul with rapture to have found
This girl so utterly discreet and sound!
I have in my house a pearl of purest honor!
She treats a love glance as a slur upon her!
A billet-doux does nothing but offend her!
By *my* hand, she returns it to the sender!
I wonder if my brother's ward, in such
A situation, would have done as much.
This proves, by heaven, that girls are what we make them.
Ho, there!

(*He knocks on Valère's door.*)

ERGASTE

Yes?

SGANARELLE

These are your master's property; take them.
Tell him that no more letters need be sent
In small gold boxes; it's most impertinent,
And he has greatly angered Isabelle.
See, it's not even been opened: he can tell
By that how low is her regard for him,
And that the prospects for his love are dim.

SCENE FIVE

VALÈRE

What were you given by that surly brute?

ERGASTE

A letter, Sir, and a gold box to boot.
He claims that you sent Isabelle this letter,
Which, he declares, has mightily upset her.
She's sent it back unopened. Come, read it, Sir.
Let's see how accurate my conjectures were.

VALÈRE, *reading*

"This letter will doubtless surprise you, and both in
my decision to write it and in the manner of its delivery
I must seem very rash indeed; but I find myself in such a
situation that I cannot observe the proprieties any longer.
My just aversion to a marriage with which I am threatened
in six days' time has made me ready to dare anything; and
in my determination to escape that bondage by whatever means
I have thought it better to turn to you than to embrace
Despair. Still, you must not think that you owe everything
to my afflicted state; it is not the predicament in which I
find myself that has given rise to my feelings for you; but

53

it hastens my avowal of them, and causes me to overstep the bounds of decorum prescribed for my sex. Whether I am soon to be yours is now entirely up to you; I wait only for a declaration of your heart's intentions before acquainting you with the resolution I have taken; but do be aware that time is pressing, and that two hearts attuned by love should need but few words to come to an understanding."

ERGASTE

Well, Sir! Was this a clever ruse, or not?
For a young girl, she lays a brilliant plot!
Love is a game, it seems, that she can play.

VALÈRE

Oh, she's adorable in every way!
This evidence of her wit and warmth of heart
Doubles my love for her, which had its start
When first her beauty caused my head to swim . . .

ERGASTE

Here comes our dupe; think what you'll say to him.

SCENE SIX

SGANARELLE, *thinking himself alone*

Ah, thrice and four times may the heavens bless
This law which bans extravagance in dress!
No more will husbands' troubles be so great,
And women's frivolous cravings will abate.
Oh, how I thank the King for such decrees,
And how I wish that, for men's further ease
Of mind, he'd ban not only lace and frills
But coquetry and its attendant ills!
I've bought this edict so that Isabelle
May read it aloud to me, and learn it well.
Some evening, when her tasks are all complete,
We'll have it for an after-supper treat.
                    (*Perceiving Valère:*)
Well, do you plan now, Mister Goldilocks,
To send more love notes in that gilded box?
You thought you'd found a young coquette who'd be
Fond of intrigue and honeyed flattery,
But what a chill response your offerings got!
Believe me, lad, you waste your powder and shot.
She's a sensible girl; it's me she loves; why aim
At one who scorns you? Go hunt for easier game.

55

VALÈRE

Indeed, your merits, which all the world admires,
Are a hopeless barrier, Sir, to my desires.
Much as I love her, it's folly on my part
To vie with you for Isabelle's hand and heart.

SGANARELLE

Quite right, it's folly.

VALÈRE

                    I wouldn't, furthermore,
Have yielded to the charms which I adore,
Had I foreseen that I was doomed to meet,
In you, a rival no man could defeat.

SGANARELLE

I quite believe you.

VALÈRE

                    I now can hope no longer,
And freely grant, Sir, that your claim's the stronger.

SGANARELLE

Well done.

[*Act Two · Scene Six*]

VALÈRE

In this, I merely do what's right,
For, Sir, your many virtues shine so bright
That I'd do wrong to take a grudging view
Of Isabelle's great tenderness toward you.

SGANARELLE

Of course.

VALÈRE

Your victory, then, I don't contest.
But, Sir, I pray you (it's the sole request
Of a poor lover whom you have overthrown,
And whose great pains are due to you alone),
I pray you, Sir, to say to Isabelle
That in these months I've spent beneath her spell
My love's been pure, and never entertained
A thought by which her honor might be pained.

SGANARELLE

Agreed.

VALÈRE

That the one thing I desired of life
Was that I might obtain her for my wife,
Till fate obstructed my desire, revealing
That she was bound to you by tenderest feeling.

SGANARELLE

Good. Good.

VALÈRE

          That, whatever happens, she must not
Think that her charms will ever be forgot;
That, let the Heavens treat me as they may,
My fate's to love her till my dying day;
And that your merits, of which I stand in awe,
Are the sole reason why I now withdraw.

SGANARELLE

Well said; I'll go at once and give her this
Message, which she will scarcely take amiss.
But if I may advise you, do your best
To drive this fruitless passion from your breast.
Farewell.

ERGASTE, *to Valère*

    What a perfect dupe!

SGANARELLE, *alone*

              It makes me sad
To see the anguish of this lovesick lad;
'Twas his misfortune to suppose that he
Could storm a fortress long since won by me.

SCENE SEVEN

SGANARELLE, ISABELLE

SGANARELLE

Never did any swain so hang his head
To see his billet-doux come back unread.
He's lost all hope, and will no longer woo you,
But begs me to convey this message to you:
That in his passion, he never entertained
A thought by which your honor might be pained,
And that the one thing he desired of life
Was that he might obtain you for his wife,
Till fate obstructed his desire, revealing
That you were bound to me by tenderest feeling;
That, whatsoever happens, you must not
Think that your charms will ever be forgot;
That, let the Heavens treat him as they may,
His fate's to love you till his dying day;
And that my merits, of which he stands in awe,
Are the sole cause which leads him to withdraw.
Those are his touching words; I cannot hate him;
He's a decent fellow, and I commiserate him.

ISABELLE, *aside*

Those sweet words but confirm my heart's surmise;
I read his pure intentions in his eyes.

59

[*Act Two · Scene Seven*]

SGANARELLE

Eh? What did you say?

ISABELLE

        I said that I'm distressed
To hear you pity a man I so detest,
And that, if you truly loved me, you would share
My rage at the affronts he's made me bear.

SGANARELLE

But he didn't know, dear, that your heart was mine;
And his intentions were so pure and fine
That one can hardly —

ISABELLE

        Is it well-intended, pray,
To seize a person, and carry her away?
Would a man of honor think it a noble course
To snatch me from you, and marry me by force?
As if I were the kind of girl who could
Survive such insults to her maidenhood!

SGANARELLE

Do you mean to tell me —

ISABELLE

        Yes; this brutish lover
Talks of abducting me, I now discover.
I don't know by what secret means he can
Have learned so very quickly of your plan

[*Act Two · Scene Seven*]

To marry me within a week or so,
Since only yesterday you let me know;
But he intends to strike at once, I find,
Before our loves and fates can be combined.

SGANARELLE

Well, this is bad indeed.

ISABELLE

Oh, no! I'm sure
He's a decent fellow, whose aims are fine and pure!

SGANARELLE

This is no joke; he's wrong in the extreme.

ISABELLE

Your mildness prompts him to this madcap scheme.
If you'd been harsh with him just now, he would
Have feared your wrath and mine, and stopped for good;
But even after his letter was returned
He hatched the shocking plot of which I've learned,
Convinced in spite of all, it would appear,
That in my heart of hearts I hold him dear,
That I am loath to wed you, and cannot wait
For him to free me from my captive state.

SGANARELLE

He's mad.

[*Act Two · Scene Seven*]

ISABELLE

With you, he knows how to disguise
His feelings, and pull the wool over your eyes.
But his fair words make sport of you, believe me.
It does, I'm forced to tell you, deeply grieve me
That after all I've done, for honor's sake,
To balk the vile advances of this rake,
I still must find myself exposed to these
Shameful designs and base conspiracies!

SGANARELLE

There, there; don't worry.

ISABELLE

              I swear, if you do not
Rebuke him fiercely for this impudent plot,
And find a way to put a stop at once
To this bold rogue's continual affronts,
I shall embrace some desperate solution
And, once for all, escape his persecution.

SGANARELLE

Come, come, my little dear, don't fret and frown;
I'll go at once and give him a dressing down.

ISABELLE

Tell him it's useless to play innocent,
That I've been fully informed of his intent,

And that, whatever he may now devise,
I challenge him to take me by surprise;
Tell him he wastes his time, and urge him to
Remember what my feelings are toward you;
And add that, lest he pay a bitter price,
He'd best not wait for me to warn him twice.

SGANARELLE

I'll say what's needful.

ISABELLE

               Show him I mean all this
By speaking it with gravest emphasis.

SGANARELLE

Yes, yes, I'll say it all, and I'll be stern.

ISABELLE

I'll wait impatiently for your return.
Please hasten back to me with all your might;
I'm desolate when you are out of sight.

[*Act Two · Scene Seven*]

SGANARELLE

Fear not, I'll soon be back with you, my sweet.
    (*Alone:*)
Was ever a girl more prudent, more discreet?
How happy I am! How fortunate to find
A wife so suited to my heart and mind!
Yes, that is how our women ought to be—
Not like some wives I know, whose coquetry
And bold amours have managed to embarrass
Their wretched mates before the whole of Paris.
    (*Knocking at Valère's door:*)
Ho there, my fine and enterprising swain!

SCENE EIGHT

VALÈRE, SGANARELLE, ERGASTE

VALÈRE

What brings you back, Sir?

SGANARELLE

Your follies, once again.

VALÈRE

What?

SGANARELLE

Come, you understand my reference.
Frankly, I thought that you had better sense.
You've hoaxed me with fine speeches, and continue
To harbor vain and foolish hopes within you.
I've wished to treat you gently, but — see here —
If this goes on, my rage will be severe.
Aren't you ashamed that you, a gentleman,
Should stoop to such skullduggery, should plan
To abduct a decent girl, and cheat her of
A marriage which would bring her joy and love?

VALÈRE

Sir, where did you hear this curious news? Do tell.

SGANARELLE

Let's not dissemble; my source is Isabelle,
Who for the last time tells you, through my voice,
That she's informed you plainly of her choice;
That she's mine, and hates this plot that you've devised;
That she'd rather die than be thus compromised,
And that there will be dire results, unless
You put an end to all this foolishness.

VALÈRE

If that is truly what she said, it seems
That there's no future for my ardent dreams:
Those plain words tell me I must yield at last
And bow before the sentence she has passed.

SGANARELLE

If? Do you doubt, then, that they came from her,
These words I've brought you as her messenger?
Would you care to hear them from her lips? I'm quite
Prepared to allow it, just to set you right.
Follow me, then, and learn from her directly
Whom she prefers, and if I spoke correctly.

SCENE NINE

ISABELLE

You've brought him here — to me? With what design?
Have you taken *his* side, and forsaken mine?
Have his merits charmed you so that I'm to be
Compelled to love him, and bear his company?

SGANARELLE

Ah, no. I'd never give you up, my precious.
But he thinks that my reports were meretricious,
That I falsified your feelings when I stated
That you were fond of me, and he was hated;
Therefore I'd have you speak to him, and dispose
Of this delusion on which his hopes repose.

ISABELLE, *to Valère*

What! When I've bared my whole soul to your eyes,
Can you still doubt where my affection lies?

VALÈRE

Madam, this gentleman's reports were such,
I own, as to surprise me very much:
Frankly, I doubted them; and this last decree,

67

Which sentences my heart to misery,
So stuns me that I dare request of you
That you repeat those words, if they were true.

ISABELLE

No sentence that I've passed should have surprised you:
Of what I feel, my plain words have advised you,
But since my judgments had both truth and strength
I don't mind stating them at greater length.
Yes, hear me, gentlemen, and believe me, too:
Fate here presents two objects to my view
Who agitate my heart with sentiments
Quite different, though equally intense.
The first, whom honor bids me choose, I deem
Worthy of all my love, all my esteem;
The other one's affection gains from me
All my resentment and antipathy.
The presence of the first is dear and sweet,
And makes my soul's felicity complete;
As for the other, my heart is seized by grim
Hatred and horror at the sight of him.
The first I long to marry, while if I
Were forced to wed the other, I'd wish to die.
But I've now said enough of what I feel,
And borne too long the pains of this ordeal;
It's time for him I love to terminate
Decisively the hopes of him I hate,
And by a happy marriage deliver me
From torments worse than death itself could be.

SGANARELLE

There, there: I'll grant your wishes, little one.

ISABELLE

I'll have no happiness till that is done.

SGANARELLE

You'll soon be happy.

ISABELLE

    It's scandalous, I know,
For a young girl to declare her passions so.

SGANARELLE

No, no.

ISABELLE

   Yet in my present state of strain
I take the liberty of being plain,
And cannot blush for the fervent things I've said
Of one to whom I feel already wed.

SGANARELLE

Of course not, sweetest angel, dearest dear.

ISABELLE

Let him now prove his love at last.

SGANARELLE

      Yes — here —
Come kiss my hand.

[*Act Two · Scene Nine*]

ISABELLE

Let him delay no more,
But speed the nuptial day I'm yearning for,
And take my promise now that none but he
Shall ever speak his marriage vows to me.
(*She pretends to embrace Sganarelle, and
gives Valère her hand to kiss.*)

SGANARELLE

Haha, my pretty duck, my pussycat!
You shall not pine for long, I promise that:
There, now! (*To Valère:*) You see, she cares for me alone.
I didn't prompt her; those words were all her own.

VALÈRE

Well, Madam, you've made your feelings clear indeed:
I grasp your wishes, and shall pay them heed.
I'll rid you very soon, you may be sure,
Of him whose presence you can not endure.

ISABELLE

Do so, and I'll be infinitely grateful;
For merely to behold him is so hateful,
So insupportable, so odious —

SGANARELLE

Now, now.

ISABELLE

I offend you, then, by speaking thus?

[*Act Two · Scene Nine*]

SGANARELLE

Oh, mercy, not in the least. But I confess
I feel some pity for the man's distress;
You put your adverse feelings too severely.

ISABELLE

At a time like this, they can't be put too clearly.

VALÈRE

Well, I'll oblige you. In three days from this date
You'll see no more the object of your hate.

ISABELLE

Thank heaven. Farewell.

SGANARELLE, *to Valère*

               I'm sorry for your pain,
But —

VALÈRE

    No, you'll not hear me whimper or complain:
In judging us, *Madame's* been most judicious,
And I'll now strive to gratify her wishes.
Farewell.

SGANARELLE

    Poor lad, he's utterly undone.
Come, I'm her other self; embrace me, son.
            (*He embraces Valère.*)

SGANARELLE

He's much to be pitied.

ISABELLE

I feel no such emotion.

SGANARELLE

In any case, I'm touched by your devotion,
My sweet, and it deserves some recompense;
A week's too long to keep you in suspense;
Tomorrow, then, shall be our wedding day.

ISABELLE

Tomorrow?

SGANARELLE

From modesty, you feign dismay,
But I well know what joy my words created,
And that you wish we were already mated.

72

[*Act Two · Scene Ten*]

ISABELLE

But —

SGANARELLE

Let's prepare for the wedding; come, be quick.

ISABELLE, *aside*

Inspire me, Heaven! I need another trick.

ACT 3

SCENE ONE

ISABELLE

ISABELLE, *alone*

Yes, death is far less dire to contemplate
Than a forced marriage to an unloved mate,
And I should not be censured, but forgiven
For any subterfuge to which I'm driven.
Time passes; night has fallen; I now must dare
To trust my fate and fortune to Valère.

SCENE TWO

SGANARELLE, ISABELLE

SGANARELLE (*Enters, muttering to himself:*)

That's done. Tomorrow, when the magistrate —

ISABELLE

Oh, Heaven!

SGANARELLE

   Is it you, dear? Where are you going so late?
You told me, when I left, that you desired
To go to your chamber, being a little tired;
You even begged that I, upon returning,
Would not disturb you till tomorrow morning.

ISABELLE

That's true, but —

SGANARELLE

   Yes?

ISABELLE

You see my hesitation;
I fear that you won't like the explanation.

SGANARELLE

Come, tell me.

ISABELLE

You'll be amazed. The reason for
My going out is sister Léonor;
She's borrowed my chamber, which she means to use
As part of a disreputable ruse.

SGANARELLE

What?

ISABELLE

Would you believe it? She loves that rogue whom we
Have just sent packing.

SGANARELLE

Valère?

ISABELLE

Yes, desperately:
I've never seen an ardor so intense;
And you may judge her passion's violence
By her coming here, at such an hour, alone,
To make the anguish of her spirit known.

79

She told me that she surely will expire
Unless she can obtain her heart's desire,
That for a year and more, Valère and she
Were fervent lovers, meeting secretly,
And that, when first they loved, they traded vows,
Each promising to become the other's spouse.

SGANARELLE

The wretched girl!

ISABELLE

    That, knowing how I'd sent
The man she worships into banishment,
She begged me to allow her, since her heart
Would break if he were ever to depart,
To bid him in my name to come tonight
And stand beneath my window, so that she might
Impersonate my voice, and in a vein
Of sweet indulgence move him to remain —
Thus using for her own ends, as you see,
The warm regard she knows he feels for me.

SGANARELLE

And do you condone —

ISABELLE

    I? No, I'm much put out.
"Sister," I said, "you're mad beyond a doubt.
'Do you not blush to throw your heart away
'On a fickle sort who changes every day,
'And shame your sex by choosing him instead
'Of the trusting man whom Heaven would have you wed?"

80

SGANARELLE

Just what the fool deserves; I'm most content.

ISABELLE

In short, with many a furious argument
I chided her behavior, and said I quite
Refused to let her use my room, tonight;
But she poured such entreaties in my ears,
And heaved such sighs, and wept so many tears,
And said so often that she would despair
Unless I granted her impassioned prayer,
That love for her compelled me to accede.
Then, to secure the witness I might need
To clear my name, I thought to ask my friend
Lucrèce, whose many virtues you commend,
To spend the night with me. But ere I could go,
Your quick return surprised me, as you know.

SGANARELLE

No! All this jugglery I won't permit.
To spite my brother, I might agree to it;
But from the street they might be seen and heard;
And she on whom my hand's to be conferred
Must be not only chaste by disposition,
And gently bred, but quite above suspicion.
Let's send this wanton girl away, and teach her —

81

[*Act Three · Scene Two*]

ISABELLE

Oh, no; you'd be too harsh with the poor creature;
And she might very justly take offense
At my betrayal of her confidence.
Since you require me to refuse my sister,
Stay here, at least, until I have dismissed her.

SGANARELLE

Well, do so, then.

ISABELLE

           Pray find some place of hiding,
And let her leave without reproach or chiding.

SGANARELLE

For love of you I'll curb my anger, dear;
But just as soon as she is out of here
I'll run and find my brother; 'twill be a rare
Pleasure to let him know of this affair.

ISABELLE

In your account, please leave my name unsaid.
Good night: when she has left, I'll go to bed.

SGANARELLE

Until tomorrow, my pet. I cannot wait
To see my brother, and tell him of his fate!
He's proven a fool, for all his glib conceit:
Not for a million would I miss this treat.

[*Act Three · Scene Two*]

ISABELLE (*Inside the house:*)

Yes, sister, I'm sorry that you're so distressed,
But I can't grant the favor you request.
The danger to my honor would be too great.
Farewell. Best hurry home; it's growing late.

SGANARELLE

She'll leave, I wager, feeling cross and sore.
For fear she may come back, I'll lock the door.

ISABELLE, *aside, as she emerges in disguise*

Help my cause, Heaven; don't abandon me.

SGANARELLE, *aside*

Where is she going? I'll follow a bit, and see.

ISABELLE, *aside*

At any rate, this dark night serves my end.

SGANARELLE, *aside*

She's gone to Valère's house! What can she intend?

SCENE THREE

VALÈRE, ISABELLE, SGANARELLE

VALÈRE, *coming out in haste*

Yes, yes; tonight, if some way can be found
To tell her . . . Who's there?

ISABELLE

Valère, don't make a sound.
You needn't go out; I'm here; it's Isabelle.

SGANARELLE, *aside*

No, you're not she; what a brazen lie you tell!
She lives by honor, whereas you flirt with shame,
And falsely have assumed her voice and name.

ISABELLE, *to Valère*

However, unless your goal is matrimony —

VALÈRE

My heart is moved by that sweet purpose only.
Tomorrow, I assure you, I shall seize
The chance to wed you in any church you please.

[*Act Three · Scene Three*]

SGANARELLE, *aside*

Poor hoodwinked fool!

VALÈRE

Come in, and have no fear;
That dupe, your guardian, cannot touch you here,
And ere I let him sunder me from you
This arm of mine will run him through and through.

SGANARELLE, *alone*

Oh, rest assured that I won't deprive you of
This shameless girl, who's so enslaved by love;
That what you've promised her does not aggrieve me,
And that I'll *make* you marry her, believe me!
Yes, he must be surprised with that young doxy:
Both as her well-respected father's proxy
And for her sister's name, I must see to it
That she avoids disgrace, if I can do it.
Ho, there!
        (He knocks at the door of a magistrate.)

SCENE FOUR

SGANARELLE, A MAGISTRATE, A NOTARY,

AN ATTENDANT WITH A LANTERN

MAGISTRATE

Yes?

SGANARELLE

Magistrate, I'm glad you're here.
You're needed, Sir, in your official gear.
Please follow me, and bring that lantern, too.

MAGISTRATE

We were going —

SGANARELLE

But this is urgent.

MAGISTRATE

What must I do?

SGANARELLE

Go in there, and take two culprits by surprise
Who should be joined by lawful marriage ties.

I know the girl: she, trusting in the vows
Of one Valère, was lured into his house.
She comes of good and noble family, yet —

MAGISTRATE

If that's your purpose, we're indeed well-met,
For we have a notary with us.

SGANARELLE

That would be you, Sir?

NOTARY

Yes, a King's notary.

MAGISTRATE

A man of honor too, Sir.

SGANARELLE

Of course. Well, use that door — tread softly, eh? —
And don't let anybody get away.
You shall be well-rewarded for this endeavor;
Don't let them try to grease your palm, however.

MAGISTRATE

What! Do you think that a jurist of my station —

SGANARELLE

I meant no slur upon your occupation.
I'll go at once and fetch my brother. Kindly
Allow your lantern bearer to walk behind me.
                    (*Aside:*)
Now, gentle brother, I'll pay you a cheery visit.
Hello!

                    (*He knocks at Ariste's door.*)

SCENE FIVE

ARISTE, SGANARELLE

ARISTE

Who's knocking? Ah there, Brother! What is it?

SGANARELLE

Come, my wise pedagogue, my agèd beau,
There are pretty doings of which you ought to know.

ARISTE

How's that?

SGANARELLE

I bring you pleasant tidings.

ARISTE

Well?

SGANARELLE

Where is your Léonor tonight, pray tell?

[*Act Three · Scene Five*]

ARISTE

Why do you ask? As I recall, she's gone
To a friend's house, for a ball.

SGANARELLE

          Ha! Well, come on
And see what sort of ball such girls prefer.

ARISTE

What are you saying?

SGANARELLE

          How well you've tutored her!
"It does no good to censure and upbraid;
'No, it's by kindness that young minds are swayed;
'It isn't bolts and bars and strict controls
'That give our wives and maidens virtuous souls;
'Too much constraint can make them misbehave,
'And a bit of freedom's what all women crave."
Well, she's been free in the extreme, I'd say,
And her virtue grows more easy every day.

ARISTE

What are you getting at? I cannot quite —

SGANARELLE

Ah, dearest elder brother, this serves you right!
I wouldn't miss it; you shall now find out
What your crazed theories have brought about.
See how these girls reflect what they've been taught;
Mine flees from gallants, yours chooses to be caught.

90

[*Act Three · Scene Five*]

ARISTE

If you won't stop riddling —

SGANARELLE

        The riddle of this affair
Is that her ball's at the house of young Valère;
That I saw her steal by night into his place,
And that she's, even now, in his embrace.

ARISTE

Who?

SGANARELLE

Léonor.

ARISTE

Please, please, let's have no jokes.

SGANARELLE

He dares dismiss my story as a hoax!
Poor fellow, I've told you — and I say once more —
That at Valère's you'll find your Léonor.
Know, too, that they were pledged to marry, well
Before he dreamt of courting Isabelle.

ARISTE

This tale's preposterous. You cannot mean it.

[*Act Three · Scene Five*]

SGANARELLE

He won't believe it, even when he's seen it!
This drives me mad. Old age without a brain
(*Tapping his forehead:*)
Is not worth much.

ARISTE

Come, Brother, do you maintain —

SGANARELLE

Lord, no! I maintain nothing. Just follow me,
And you'll be freed from all uncertainty.
You'll see if I lie, and if it isn't so
That their troths were plighted more than a year ago.

ARISTE

Does it seem likely that she would embark
On such a course, and leave *me* in the dark,
When, all her life, I've looked with an entire
Indulgence on her every young desire,
And promised always that I'd not prevent
Her heart from freely following its bent?

SGANARELLE

Come, let your own eyes judge how matters stand.
A magistrate and notary are on hand:
The promised marriage should at once take place,
I think, to rescue her from more disgrace.
You, I assume, care something for your honor,
And would not wed her with this stain upon her —

[*Act Three* · *Scene Five*]

Unless you fancy that your liberal vision
And fine ideas could save you from derision.

ARISTE

To claim another's heart against her will
Is something I would scorn to do. But still
I'm not convinced that—

SGANARELLE

How you do run on!
Let's go, or we'll be chattering here till dawn.

93

SCENE SIX

MAGISTRATE

There's no need for compulsion, gentlemen;
If all you want is to see them married, then
I here and now can give you peace of mind.
Both parties, I am told, are so inclined,
And here is a signed statement from Valère
That he means to wed the girl now in his care.

ARISTE

And the girl's — ?

MAGISTRATE

          Locked in, and won't come out unless
You grant their wish for wedded happiness.

SCENE SEVEN

VALÈRE, THE MAGISTRATE, THE NOTARY, SGANARELLE, ARISTE

VALÈRE, *at the window of his house*

No, gentlemen; none shall enter here till you've
Assured me formally that you approve.
You know me, Sirs; I've done what I must do
And signed the instrument they'll show to you.
If you are willing, then, for us to marry,
Your signatures are all that's necessary;
If not, you'll have to take my life before
You rob me of the one whom I adore.

SGANARELLE

No, we'll not rob you; set your mind at rest.
                    (*Sotto voce, aside:*)
He still believes that Isabelle is his guest:
Well, let him think it.

ARISTE, *to Valère*

But is it Léonor — ?

SGANARELLE, *to Ariste*

Be quiet.

95

ARISTE

But —

SGANARELLE

Hush.

ARISTE

I want to know —

SGANARELLE

Once more,
Will you be quiet?

VALÈRE

In any case, good Sirs,
Isabelle has my pledge, as I have hers.
Do think it over: I'm not so poor a catch
That you should make objection to the match.

ARISTE, *to Sganarelle*

The name he said was —

SGANARELLE

Quiet! When this is through,
You shall know everything. (*To Valère:*) Yes, without more ado,
We both agree that you shall be the spouse
Of her who is at present in your house.

MAGISTRATE

Just how this contract puts it, to the letter.
The name's left blank, because we've not yet met her.
Sign here. The girl can do so by and by.

VALÈRE

I agree to that.

SGANARELLE

With my whole heart, so do I.
(*Aside:*)
What a laugh I soon shall have! (*To Ariste:*) Sign, Brother dear;
You should go first.

ARISTE

All this is so unclear —

SGANARELLE

Sign, sign, you idiot! What are you waiting for?

ARISTE

He speaks of Isabelle, you of Léonor.

SGANARELLE

What if it's she? Are you not willing, Brother,
To let these two keep faith with one another?

[*Act Three · Scene Seven*]

ARISTE

Surely.

SGANARELLE

Then sign, and I shall do the same.

ARISTE

Very well; but I'm baffled.

SGANARELLE

I'll soon explain the game.

MAGISTRATE

We shall return, Sirs.
(*Exeunt Magistrate and Notary into Valère's house.*)

SGANARELLE

Now then, I'll reveal
Some secrets to you.
(*They retire to the back of the stage.*)

SCENE EIGHT

LÉONOR, SGANARELLE, ARISTE, LISETTE

LÉONOR

Oh, what a grim ordeal!
I find those young men tiresome, one and all.
On their account, I slipped away from the ball.

LISETTE

They all try hard to please you, and be engaging.

LÉONOR

Nevertheless, I find their talk enraging.
I'd rather hear the simplest common sense
Than all that empty prattle they dispense.
They think their blond wigs dazzle every eye,
And that they're fearfully witty when they try
To tease one, in a bright, malicious fashion,
About the limits of an old man's passion.
But I prefer an old man's kindly zeal
To the giddy transports young men claim to feel.
Ah! Don't I see — ?

[*Act Three · Scene Eight*]

SGANARELLE, *to Ariste*

Well, Brother, now you know.
(*Perceiving Léonor:*)
But look! She's coming, with her maid in tow.

ARISTE

Léonor, I am not angry, but I'm pained:
You know your freedom's never been constrained,
And that you've long been promised, on my part,
Full liberty in matters of the heart.
Yet, as if doubtful that I would approve,
You've gone behind my back to pledge your love.
I don't regret my leniency, but such
Mistrustful conduct hurts me very much,
And what you've done is not a fair return
For my affection and my warm concern.

LÉONOR

I cannot guess to what your words refer;
My feelings, though, are what they always were,
And my regard for you is firm and strong.
I could not love another, and do you wrong.
If you would see my chief wish satisfied,
Say that tomorrow I may be your bride.

ARISTE

Then, Brother, on what foundation did you base —

[*Act Three · Scene Eight*]

SGANARELLE

What! Didn't you come, just now, from Valère's place?
Didn't you tell your sister, just today,
That, a year ago, he stole your heart away?

LÉONOR

Tell me, who took the trouble to devise
Such tales about me, and spin such pretty lies?

SCENE NINE

ISABELLE, VALÈRE, THE MAGISTRATE, THE NOTARY,

ERGASTE, LISETTE, LÉONOR, SGANARELLE, ARISTE

ISABELLE

Sister, I fear I've taken liberties
With your good name; will you forgive me, please?
Under the pressure of a sudden crisis
I've stooped, today, to certain low devices:
By your example I am put to shame;
But fortune did not treat us both the same.
(*To Sganarelle:*)
Sir, I shall offer no apologies tò you;
It is a service, not a wrong, I do you.
The Heavens did not design us to be wed:
I felt unworthy of you, and instead
Of making you an undeserving wife,
I chose another man to share my life.

VALÈRE, *to Sganarelle*

I count it, Sir, my greatest joy and pride
That from your hands I have received my bride.

ARISTE

Best take this quietly, Brother; your own extreme
Behavior forced these two to plot and scheme,

102

[*Act Three · Scene Nine*]

And it will be your sad lot, I foresee,
To be a dupe who gets no sympathy.

LISETTE

Well, I'm delighted. This clever trick's a just
Reward for his suspicion and mistrust.

LÉONOR

I'm not sure that their trick deserves applause,
But I can't blame them, for they had good cause.

ERGASTE

He's a born cuckold, and lucky to get out
Of marriage before his horns began to sprout.

SGANARELLE, *emerging from his stupefaction*

No, I can't fathom it; I'm overcome;
Such treachery is too deep for me to plumb;
I can't believe that Satan himself could be
As wicked as this jade has been to me.
I would have sworn she could not do amiss;
Let no man trust a woman, after this!
The best of them are guileful and perverse;
Their breed was made to be creation's curse.
The Devil take them all! I hereby sever
Relations with their faithless sex forever.

ERGASTE

Good.

[*Act Three* · *Scene Nine*]

ARISTE

Come to my house, friends. Tomorrow we'll assuage,
As best we can, my brother's pain and rage.

LISETTE, *to the audience*

D'you know any churlish husbands? If you do,
Send them to us: we'll teach them a thing or two.